THE LIFE OF THE WORLD'S CUTEST DOG

by

J. H. Lee

Photography by

Gretchen LeMaistre

CHRONICLE BOOKS

SAN FRANCISCO

Library of Congress Cataloging-in-Publication Data available.

ISBN: 978-1-4521-0306-8

Manufactured in China
Designed by Suzanne LaGasa
Photographed by Gretchen LeMaistre

10 9 8

Chronicle Books
680 Second Street
San Francisco, California 94107
www.chroniclebooks.com

MIX
Paper from
responsible sources
FSC® C104723

Hello, my name is Boo. This is my life.

I like to lounge around the house.

I find my best friend Buddy.

We have family time to discuss our plans.

We play hide-and-seek.

But I'm not very good at it.

I love getting into snug spaces.

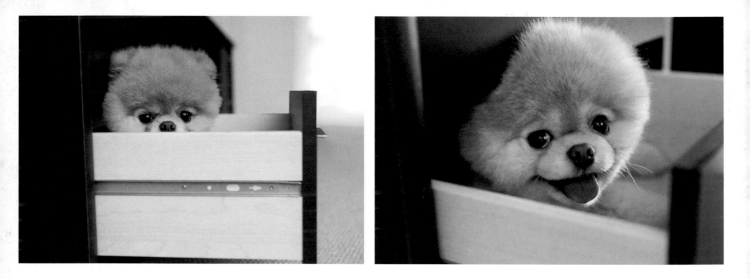

Peekaboo!

Every day, I make important wardrobe decisions.

Casual pup

Glam pup

Urban pup

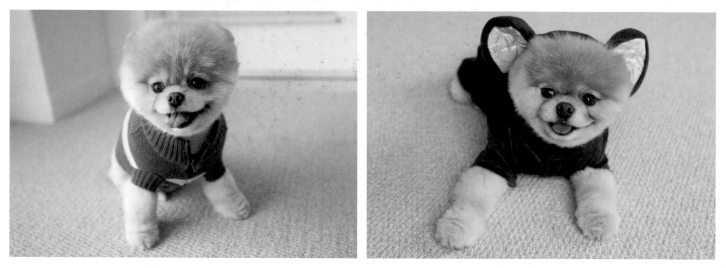

Preppy pup Monkey pup

Sporty pup

This is my outdoor walking outfit.

Sometimes I escape the walking outfit, and I take off!

This is my naked-in-the-grass look.

I also sport my running suit.

Even when I don't plan on running.

Camouflage comes in handy when I'm out in the wild.

Dog waste is not a fertilizer

**PLEASE KEEP DOGS
OFF THE LAWN**

Thank You

I wind down with a little mental exercise.

And I hang out with Buddy.

When it's time to eat, I know to say please.

And thank you.

Treats always follow.

Yum!

Nothing says "I'm hungry" like smiling by an empty bowl.

Meal time ends with a drink from my favorite mug.

Eating is obviously followed by sleeping. This is where I hibernate.

And this is where I nap.

Buddy likes to sneak in.

Sometimes I nap in style.

Fresh laundry makes a great nap-time blanket.

Blanket burritos are the best.

On my birthday I get special presents.

Then we play!

Cutie camouflage

Can you spot me?

I would be the one with the giant head.

Then we do more of what we do best: nap!

Buddy and I play together.

Sometimes I soak in the sun by the pool.

I work on my tan.

Time to head back home!

Checking myself out.

The sink is another nice snug spot.

I can be a little naughty.

Bath time?

Bathing is not one of the highlights of my day.

Duckie doesn't understand personal space.

This is not a good look for me.

After a long day, it's time for my favorite thing again: sleep!

Buddy tries to get on my side of the bed.

But we find that this way usually works best.

I get sleepy eyes and snuggle into the covers.

Good night!

Sleep tight.

I dedicate this book to my best friend **Buddy**.
Thank you for always being by my side and
giving me a lead to follow.

I'd also like to thank my many **Facebook fans**
for loving a silly dog with a funny haircut.
I hope you enjoyed my story!